K M Murphy was born in 1980 in Stirling, Scotland, and was brought up in a small mining village.

Her writing career began when she woke up one day and decided, "I'm going to write a book today."

Although kept busy with a part-time job in education, another in bridal retail, doing voluntary work and being a mum and wife, she feels like she has most definitely found a new passion in writing.

Taking inspiration from her childhood and life experiences, she writes with a very down to earth and refreshingly honest tone.

Her other great loves in life are her family and friends, singing and dancing, anything sparkly, Christmas time, flavoured gins and yankee candles.

For all brides past, and brides to be.

K M Murphy

SAY AYE TAE THE FROCK

AUSTIN MACAULEY PUBLISHERS™

LONDON · CAMBRIDGE · NEW YORK · SHARJAH

A CIP catalogue record for this title is available from the British Library.

ISBN 9781398422650 (Paperback)
ISBN 9781398422667 (ePub e-book)

www.austinmacauley.com

First Published 2022
Austin Macauley Publishers Ltd®
1 Canada Square
Canary Wharf
London
E14 5AA

Thanks to Dianne, Lynne and my wonderful husband, for your continued support throughout the writing of my first book.

Table of Contents

Disclaimer

Say Aye Tae the Frock reflects the authors recollections of experiences over a period of time. Names and characteristics have been changed. Some events have been compressed or exaggerated and some dialogues have been recreated.

Introduction

I've been obsessed by weddings and the idea of being a bride, since I was a little girl. So when my own big day came, I just revelled in it. It couldn't have been more perfect. I loved everything about it, even all the planning and preparation on the lead up to the big event. I've always been interested and drawn to anything wedding related. I love looking at wedding photos and still can't walk by a bridal shop without stopping to have a look.

So I feel very privileged that for the past eight years I have been working part-time in the bridal industry (My dream job, really). It's been wonderful being involved in wedding fayres, catwalks and to be able to help brides choose their dresses for their special day. It's been such a pleasure to be a small part of helping brides create their vision for their weddings.

Every bride and every appointment is completely different and some appointments were unforgettable. Not only were the brides unforgettable but the stories and the journeys they had leading up to the big day.

There have been so many memorable moments that I've been a part of that I decided to note them down. This is what has led me to writing: *Say Aye Tae the Frock*.

This book has been put together based on real life stories to give a true insight into what really goes on in a bridal changing room. There have been tears, laughs, tantrums, nerves, hysteria and moments of pure joy.

Here are my favourite stories.

Bride Tribes and Entourages

When the shop door opens and in pours a bride with what seems like everyone and their auntie!

Some brides like to keep their supportive people to a minimum, when choosing their dress, while others like to bring the entire clan!

So bride tribes and entourages now include a wide range of chosen ones. From friends, mums, mum in laws, sisters, babies, aunties, grans, children, dads, brothers, granddads, even husbands to be. I've seen the lot.

Appointments can vary a great deal. From quiet and personal to high energy and noisy. It really does depend on the members of the group. Some appointments can even feel like a pre-wedding party.

Hangover Hannah

It was on such an occasion when I met Amy and Hannah. One bride to be and one extremely hungover bridesmaid. Also, along with them were mum, mum in law, gran, two sisters and a friend. *Let the fun begin* I thought.

It was a Sunday morning appointment and everyone seemed bright and enthusiastic to see Amy in the wedding dresses. I didn't really notice Hannah at first as she was quieter than the rest of the group. I was about to find out why.

The girls had picked out dresses for Amy to try and I started helping Amy into a dress in the changing room. Amy picked a dress quite quickly during her appointment and was confident she'd found the one.

Everyone was admiring her as she was standing in her chosen dress. During this admiration of Amy, Hannah had started to edge towards the door. I thought maybe to get some air as it can get hot with a lot of people close together, during an appointment.

The other girls were calling to Hannah to come and see Amy in this dress. This now got the attention of the rest of the group and led them to wondering what on earth Hannah was up to? *What could be more important than Amy's dress at this precise moment in time?* Hannah slowly walked over with a look on her face like her world was about to end. She'd also turned the most awful shade of yellowy/green I've ever seen. Everyone fixed on Hannah waiting to hear what she was going to say. Before I could get the words out, *are you ok?* there it came!

She shouted, "I'm going to be sick!" Both hands covering her mouth as she started to retch with watery sick spraying through her fingers, as she ran out of the shop.

Other girls in the group jumped to guard Amy in her dress as she looked on horrified, standing there in her dream dress which was almost showered in sick!

A few girls ran out after Hannah, who was swiftly dealt with, and put into a car until Amy's appointment was finished.

Amy's mum and grans faces were a picture!

Amy got her dream dress though and Hannah was still allowed to be a bridesmaid.

So maybe a Sunday morning appointment is not the best idea for some girls.

Sticky Fingers

This was a very different entourage, as the main members of it were all under two years old.

Now, I know it's difficult to get childcare at times, and I've loved getting to meet the babies and children of the brides to be, but nothing like adding a little stress to your appointment.

Mandy decided to bring her two friends and their children as well as her own child. I immediately thought *this could get messy.*

It was a rainy day so the girls were quickly trying to get into the shop with their prams, not taking into account that wet, muddy pram wheels make lovely big tram lines over brand new wedding dress skirts! So, I quickly tried to rescue the dresses on mannequins from being mowed over and helped the girls arrange the prams in the best, safest place possible. It's not a huge bridal shop so there's not a lot of extra space. Three little children all under two, all wide awake and full of smiles, sitting in their prams quite happily.

So we started getting Mandy into some wedding dresses and she was looking great. Unbeknown to me, while I was in the changing room with Mandy, the two friends were giving the children a little snack and a drink to keep them happy. Chocolate was the snack of choice. Now, wedding dresses and chocolate don't usually go together, but the kids were in their prams so I thought, *it'll be fine*.

While we were changing into the next dress, I could hardly concentrate on Mandy for wondering what the chocolate covered children were doing. Then to my horror I heard the dreaded words from outside the changing room, "Do you want out of your pram a little while?" I came out of the changing room, with Mandy in a pristine satin wedding gown, to find the three children sitting on the sofas with the other two mums. And that's when it happened.

When Mandy's child saw her standing in the dress she jumped off the sofa to give her mum a big hug and face planted right onto the front of the dress. Oh yes, her face and hands were covered in chocolate. Everyone gasped and shouted *Oh no!* Mandy lifted up her little girl into the air at arm's length to stop any more damage while the other girls looked for wipes to clean up the children.

Poor Mandy, standing there in a beautiful dress with her chocolate dripping child.

She was furious with her friends for giving the children chocolate in the first place, and then for letting them out their prams. I have to say, I did agree with her. There were lots of apologies while trying to clean up and get Mandy out of her dress. Once things had settled down, Mandy said, "I don't think it was a good idea to bring the children." *You think!* I thought to myself.

Needless to say, Mandy didn't find her perfect dress that day and we never saw her again.

So for future reference girls, chocolate and wedding dresses just don't mix.

Hey Brother

This was one of the quieter appointments. No big entourage, but it was a surprise guest appearance that was to make it become memorable.

Erin arrived for her appointment with her two friends, Louise and Katy, who were to be her bridesmaids. They were looking forward to seeing Erin in the dresses.

Erin had explained that she had previously thought of going abroad to get married due to family circumstances, but was convinced by family members and friends to get married closer to home.

Tragically, Erin lost both her parents in a road traffic accident when she was three years old. She and her twin brother, James, were brought up by their grandparents.

She didn't want a big wedding or a lot of fuss. She described herself as someone who didn't like all the attention focused on her or to be in the limelight. She didn't seem like a ball gown kind of girl.

Louise and Katy were a great help to Erin, choosing dresses for her to try. As I got busy helping Erin in and out of the dresses, I noticed, as I was in and out of the changing room, that Louise had got busy on her phone. She was discreetly showing Katy all the texts she was sending and receiving.

Erin had now found a dress she really liked, and stood in it for a while taking it all in. While Katy kept her busy in the dress, trying on headpieces and veils, Louise asked me if I could show her to the bathroom. It was so that she could be out of ear shot of Erin, to tell me that Erin was about to have a surprise visitor arrive at the appointment. Louise had been texting Erin's brother, James, as he was keen to come and surprise her and see her in her dress.

I couldn't help thinking about the two of them growing up and never having known their parents. At special moments like this it seems all the more difficult.

We went back to join Erin and Katy and they had decided to try on one more dress. Really, just to allow James time to get here. Erin wasn't keen on the next dress so I got her back into the favourite. This was definitely the one for Erin: simple, elegant and feminine. It was a soft flowing organza material with a delicate illusion neckline and illusion back with lace detailing. She looked so pretty in it. We were trying veils on her and she had her back to the door when it opened.

James, it would appear would be perfectly happy being centre of attention. He marched into the shop with a massive bouquet of flowers shouting, *Hello ma sister! did u think you were sneaking away without letting me in on this* as he walked towards her and gave her a big cuddle. Erin was speechless and Louise and Katy beamed, happy they'd pulled off the surprise. It really was a lovely moment. He looked exactly like her, but a completely different personality. James continued, "Aw, you're just lovely hen. Let me see you, what a gorgeous wee bride." He then proceeded to whisk Erin up off her feet and waltz her all around the shop singing, "You're getting married in the morning," at the pitch of his voice. Hilarious!

Erin was shocked but delighted to see him. As were we all, what a moment. He had one more surprise for Erin though, he turned to us and said, "I'll be paying for Erin's dress and she's to get everything she wants, so just sort her out girls." Erin tried to protest saying it was too much but he had made up his mind. He left before she could say anymore shouting, "See you later girls!"

It was a really lovely moment, such a mixture of emotions. What a lovely gesture to make for his sister. You could clearly see he just adored her. Also, Erin had two fantastic friends who took pleasure in seeing her happy.

It got me thinking you really do need to treasure the loved ones you have in your life.

So whether it be a large group or a chosen few, it would seem anything can happen during a bridal appointment.

Wishing You Health

Getting married symbolises the start of a new life together for the happy couple. Most couples enter into marriage, hopeful of a long and happy future together. Some brides enter into marriage, uncertain of their futures as they are not blessed with health on their sides.

These brides were inspirational, tissues at the ready.

The Big C

Having lost a loved one to cancer myself, I know the pain and devastation it causes to those suffering, and then also to those who are left behind.

Kerry was a young bride in her twenties. She had already been diagnosed with breast cancer and undergone major surgery by the time she started planning her wedding. Not the typical experiences of your average girl in her twenties.

Kerry's mum and gran joined her at her appointment. I could see Kerry's gran and mum were very protective of Kerry, *no wonder*, I thought with everything she was going through. They just wanted to take care of her and for her to be happy. Faced with the type of illness Kerry had, I can only imagine how difficult it was for Kerry's family to remain strong for her. Sometimes it can be hard to 'Put on a brave face'.

Kerry showed no sign of illness at her appointment and if she hadn't told me about her operation, I wouldn't have noticed any difference in her. She was such a positive, genuine and bright person. She made it easy to forget what she had already been through and was still going through, treatments every month and the possibility of more operations before the big day. It was unbelievable that this girl was dealing with so much and still had such a positive outlook, she really was amazing.

Kerry really enjoyed trying on all the dresses. She also looked stunning in every dress I put her in. Her mum and gran just sat and admired her, and were happy she was enjoying it all. I could see they looked tearful but were trying not to let it show. Then Kerry's gran started to shake her head and said, "It's just not right, just a young girl."

Kerry said, "Come on now gran, no tears, this is a happy day."

"I know, I know—I'm sorry hen, I just canny help it. I should be at the end of my life and you should be at the start of yours." I was finding it really difficult to remain professional and not get emotional myself. Seeing Kerry's gran like that, I thought their poor hearts must be breaking seeing Kerry today.

Kerry's mum managed to lighten things up and got the focus back to Kerry in the dresses. Kerry's next try was to be her dream dress and she was delighted with her choice. She chose a fitted fishtail style with lace straps, heavily embellished body with a sparkly tulle skirt. Finished off with a fingertip single tier veil with sparkly edging. It definitely had the wow factor. She was now feeling really excited and looking forward to her special day.

Kerry and her family left all, giving me big cuddles and thanking me for making their experience so lovely. My emotions were shattered when they left, I couldn't stop thinking about them. I still do, often. I felt happy though that I was able to help Kerry find her dress.

Kerry was an inspiration to me because she reminded me of how precious life is and that your health should never be taken for granted.

Designer Bags

I had previously dressed a few girls who have had colostomy bags or stomas fitted. So when Gillian arrived for her appointment, I was prepared and ready to be sensitive around the area when helping to dress her. I needn't have worried.

She arrived for her appointment with her sister Sandra, and I could immediately see she was a bright and happy person.

Gillian became memorable to me because of her attitude to life. She was one of those girls who have the amazing ability to be able to laugh at herself and not take life too seriously. I always imagined this would be such a difficult thing to do when you have health concerns.

She talked openly about her health problem. It wasn't going to be something that would hold her back or stop her from being herself. I discovered early on in the appointment that Gillian was a humorous kind of girl, cracked plenty of jokes and liked a laugh. She even made references to her stoma calling it her, *Gucci pouch!* You know that way you're not sure if you should laugh as I didn't want to seem disrespectful, but she was funny.

Sandra then added, "Aye, there's a gap in the market there, Gucci must not be interested in making designer stoma bags!" I could feel myself getting ridiculous as I started to envision Gucci's next catwalk collection with accessories! I thought I'd better get Gillian into some dresses before we all lose the plot.

Clearly, Gillian was not overly self-conscious of her health problem. She had great fun trying on the dresses and confidently paraded about in them. Sandra was a good help to Gillian choosing dresses for her to try, and she gave Gillian an honest, but helpful, opinion on how she thought she looked in them. Gillian found her perfect dress that day. She chose an A line shape with illusion neck and back. It also had a beautiful lace overlay on the skirt which glinted when she moved. It was a great fit, really suited her figure and was manageable for her medical needs. So it was ticking all the boxes. Sandra agreed that she looked gorgeous in it.

Gillian was delighted with her dress and she said it made her feel like she didn't have any medical issues, but it was Gillian that made it seem that she didn't have any medical issues.

She was such a bright and bubbly person, a delight to be around. I'm sure Gillian had a ball on her wedding day.

Gillian's attitude to life put those who complain about everything to shame. We would all do good to lighten up a little, life's too short.

Wearing a Wire

Jess was memorable to me because she was a classic case of a girl who had lost her confidence due to illness and didn't believe she could look beautiful for her big day.

Jess had undergone multiple operations and still had lines and tubes fitted for medication.

She arrived for her appointment with her bride tribe, a great bunch of girls including friends, mum and gran. Jess had no idea of what she liked in a dress or what she would suit. She just kept saying, "I don't think anything will fit me."

I was determined to show her how beautiful she was and give her a wonderful bridal experience. The girls helped me pick out some dresses for Jess.

We tried on a few and she was immediately and pleasantly surprised by how she looked and felt in them. Even a wee smile starting to appear. I was glad that Jess was starting to see that there would be plenty of options for her. With every dress change, she was enjoying her appointment more and more. She tried on an A-line dress, a fit and flare, a fishtail, bohemian style and ball gowns. She even tried on some veils and tiaras. Her family were so happy to see her enjoying herself.

Then came the princess moment. Jess stepped out of the changing room in a full ball gown style dress with train and sparkly lace detail all over, cathedral length veil with lace edging finished off with a beautiful sparkly tiara. Everyone was quiet at first waiting on Jess's reaction. Then came the gasps, squeals, oh my gods and tears. Jess beamed and loved the dress. She started to cry, happy tears and said it was the one.

She said, "I'm crying because I never thought I would feel this good." Totally delighted for her and one of my favourite Cinderella moments.

These girls were amazing and unforgettable for me. With all they have had to and might still have to endure. They are a reminder that illness is no respecter of age and that we have to make each day count.

I wish them all health, wealth and happiness for the future.

Tears and Tantrums

A bridal appointment can be a very emotional time for the bride to be. With so many different factors adding to their stress levels before the big day, this can often peak during their bridal appointment or when they find the 'dream dress'.

These brides' emotions definitely over-spilled during their appointments.

Picture Perfect

Not every girl is blessed to have her parents present on her wedding day. Laura's wedding had been postponed when, sadly, she lost her mother to illness. Debating whether or not to still get married at all, she decided to set another date as her mum would have hated for her not to have her special day.

Laura had a style in mind, she wanted quite a bohemian floaty looking dress. She brought her sister and auntie along for support, and started to look through the dresses.

Laura previously had the chance to share pictures of wedding dresses with her mum that she liked, so with that in mind we tried to create that look for her.

After a few tries Laura kept talking about a particular dress that she had shown her mum in a magazine, but unfortunately, she couldn't see what she was describing in the shop.

It was at that point that her sister started to become quite tearful and produced an envelope from her bag and said, "I've got something for you," she said. "It's from mum. She gave this to me and made me promise that when we go wedding dress shopping to give this to you."

Not even knowing what was in the envelope, Laura started to get upset at the thought of her mum leaving her something to be opened at this special moment.

So Laura took a minute, settled herself and opened the envelope. There it was, the picture from the magazine of Laura's dream dress! By this point I think everyone in the shop was crying including myself. There was also a little note inside which read *I hope you find your perfect dress my beautiful girl, love mum.* Tears flowing as you can imagine.

I had a look at the picture and I knew exactly what dress it was. I also knew it had been discontinued and we couldn't order it anymore. *Oh God,* I thought, how can I tell her this.

I excused myself for a minute and pretended I needed a drink of water, and started frantically looking through all the stock in the back room, desperately trying to see if we still had the sample dress. I think I was making more mess than anything else to be honest. After looking for a while I decided it was time to give the girls the dreaded news. I started to explain how it was discontinued and I could phone some other shops to see if they had it.

Then I remembered, a large cardboard box, mostly hidden by underskirts in the stock room. So I said, "Wait a minute, there's one more thing I need to check." I brought the box through to the girls and opened it in front of them.

Now, I don't know if the angels were on our side that day but I like to think Laura's mum had a hand in it. There was the dress! Under some spare material and veils. Packed away for the next sale event. I pulled it out and, yes, it was definitely the one. I don't know who was more happy—Laura and her family or me.

Laura tried on the dress and it was an almost perfect fit. Not sure if I believe in miracles but I'm a strong believer in, "if it's for you, it'll not go by you." This dress was definitely meant for Laura.

Freak Out!

As well as having tears at appointments, I've learned that other emotions can take on a very different form when being pushed to the limit. When Sharon arrived for her appointment with her mum, I could immediately sense there was a bit of tension. When I asked Sharon what style she liked and had been trying on, her mum started to tell me what she liked Sharon in. Sharon rolled her eyes at me and tried again to tell me the style she really liked and was looking for: a fit and flare gown with straps and lace detail.

Meanwhile her mum got busy pulling out every strapless ball gown she could find, with enough glitter and sparkles on them to sink a ship. With Sharon trying to tell her, "I've told you, I don't like the big ball gown dresses."

So Sharon decided for the sake of peace to leave two ball gowns of her mum's choice on the rail to be tried on.

I got Sharon into her first dress, which was a fit and flare style, which she loved and really suited her shape. It had delicate lace straps with lace detail that continued throughout the dress and train. Her mum didn't hold back on expressing her dislike for everything about the dress, including Sharon's figure in it. I tried to mediate and calm the situation by saying it's all about how Sharon feels in the dress and it really should be her choice.

With her mum persisting to see her in another ball gown, Sharon agreed to try one on. Sharon emerged from the changing room in a dress about as wide as she was tall—it was huge. The skirt was layered with ruffles of sparkly tulle with a heavily embellished corset back bodice. Sharon's mum was squealing with delight and Sharon's face was tripping her. Sharon clearly was not comfortable and wanted to take the dress off but her mum kept going on about, how good she looked in it, how she looked thinner in it and how she didn't look like a 'real' bride in the other style.

I could see Sharon was starting to get a bit red about the face and neck, and wasn't sure if she was angry or about to cry. Her mum was still too busy going on about the ball gowns to notice. Her mum finally stopped talking at her and said, "So what do you think Sharon?" I don't think anyone would have been prepared for the torrent of expletives that was about to be her response. "I'll tell you what I fucking think," said Sharon. "I'm sick of hearing about fucking ball gowns and what you think suits me. I've told you a hundred times, I don't like FUCKING BALL GOWNS!"

Her mum stood there in shock with her mouth open and managed to stutter out, "That's enough Sharon—"

Sharon responded, "Oh, I haven't even started. This is my wedding, not yours, and I'm going to wear what I fucking like and I don't care what anyone thinks!"

I slowly backed away behind a curtain of the changing room. I hid for a few moments thinking, *I'm going to have to separate this pair!* I chose my moment to emerge again and Sharon turned to me and said, "Can you get me out this fucking dress, please."

"Nae bother," was my response while trying not to laugh at the serial situation I found myself in. Even with her choice of language, I found it difficult to take her upset seriously while she was standing there in a humungous dress.

Her mum didn't say much after that and both Sharon and her mum left with Sharon saying, "I'll be back on my own."

A little lesson to be learned here, push a bride to be to the limit and feel the wrath! So mums, let your girl have her day, it's hers not yours.

Oh Baby

Lucy's appointment started like any other. Select people with her for opinions and support who all seemed positive and looking forward to seeing Lucy in the dresses. Lucy brought along her mum, auntie, sister and a friend. Out of all the people in the group, Lucy seemed the quietest and calmest. She didn't have any particular style in mind and she was happy to take advice and try on all the styles.

On Lucy's appointment sheet, it said her wedding was still 18 months away so plenty of time from an ordering point of view. Lucy seemed determined to find her dress today and only wanted to try on dresses that she could take away today, even though this would limit her options. Her mum was trying to convince her that she had plenty of time and not to rush into anything. Saying, "I wish you would just take your time. You don't need to make a definite decision today."

Lucy started to try on the dresses. First a lace v neck with A-line skirt, then a duchess satin strapless dress with a sparkly belt. Next, a more fitted dress with beaded straps and a long train. Lucy wasn't feeling particularly special in any of them. Lucy then started to feel a bit stressed and she got tearful, her mum was frustrated that she wouldn't just take her time and order a new dress.

Then Lucy got very upset and the tears flowed. We all thought she was just a bit overwhelmed. Then I started to have the fear that she was going to say something awful had happened. You know that way you can't judge if this is going to be good or bad news. I was dying to shout *What is it? Just tell us!*

She managed to talk through the tears and said to everyone, "I need to find a dress today because the wedding's not in 18 months. We've moved the date, and it's in four months because I'm pregnant!"

There was a mixture of tears and squeals of joy. Her mum leapt up to hold her, everyone was delighted. No-one expected the news or could believe she'd kept it a secret for so long. So, not only a wedding to look forward to but a baby as well.

It was lovely to be a part of her special announcement—I don't think I'll hear one like that again.

So as you've heard there's a range of reasons as to why emotions can run high for our brides to be. I think you'd agree,

"It's been emotional."

Rogue Bridesmaids

Being asked to be a bridesmaid is considered an honour bestowed upon family members and friends, of the bride to be. Delighted to be chosen and be such a big part of the special day. Choosing the dresses together is an important part of being a bridesmaid, and as an enthusiastic bridesmaid you want to help and support the bride in her decision making. Well most bridesmaids do—

These are the bridesmaids that are memorable for all the wrong reasons.

Hyper Annie

Now, I do fall into this category slightly myself. I have been known to get a bit excitable from time to time but not to Annie's extent! (I'm sure those of you who know me the words, pot, kettle and black will have sprung to mind!).

Enthusiasm wasn't Annie's problem, she had it in abundance. She probably had enough energy to share out with everyone in the room and have loads left.

The bride to be, Sarah, was quiet by nature, soft spoken and shy. Opposite end of the scale from her friend Annie.

Annie bounced into the shop ahead of everyone and seemed like a riot from the get go. Like she'd had a wee red bull breakfast to herself. Annie also had really bouncy curly hair (like a head full of coiled springs!), which matched her personality, perfectly.

She was with two other bridesmaids, Sarah and Sarah's mum. They were in to try on bridesmaid dresses so I could understand Annie's excitement. Annie immediately got onto looking through the bridesmaid's dresses and commenting loudly on every dress i.e. "check this out Sarah, this colours awful. Oh my God! What about this blue one Sarah?" Poor Sarah already looked quite drained with her. I actually found her antics quite funny but maybe more manageable in small doses.

We got onto trying on the dresses and, of course, Annie had plenty to say. She burst out of the changing room, "Tah Dah," with every dress change and commented continuously about how she thought they all looked in them, and made decisions for everyone based on her opinion. Annie got excited as she talked, and she talked louder as she became more excited. I actually thought at one point she was going to start hyperventilating! She was totally taking over the appointment like a runaway train.

Poor Sarah couldn't get a word in. I tried to intervene a few times and asked what Sarah thought. I could see Sarah was struggling to get her thoughts across, as she was now distracted by Annie doing a full dance routine in her dress, including flossing and twerking moves while shouting, "These are my dance moves for the wedding, Sarah!" Sarah just looked at her mum and burst into tears and said, "You'll have to speak to her—she's freaking me out."

Sarah's mum took Annie to one side for a quiet word while I continued with the other bridesmaids and Sarah. After

Sarah's mum had scraped Annie down from the ceiling, and possibly gave her a tranquiliser, she did settle down slightly. We all needed paracetamol after that appointment. I could feel my adrenalin levels rising just watching her. Not surprising really, that it all got too much for Sarah.

Yeah so enthusiasm is great, girls, but know when to reel it in.

Twisted Sister

I don't have a sister so I don't have first-hand experience of growing up with a sister and forming that special bond. I do know, and have experienced, that not all sisters see eye to eye.

Stacey was to be chief bridesmaid for her sister, Elaine, along with two other friends as bridesmaids.

The girls arrived and seemed hopeful that they would get their dresses picked and ordered that day. Stacey, it would seem had other ideas. You know one of those people if you said white they'd say black, well that was the vibe I was getting from her. I don't think she smiled once throughout the appointment—she almost had a kinda sneer to her facial expression. I could sense that Elaine was anxious about her already.

As suspected, the negativity continued. Stacey liked nothing that the other girls liked and had no interest in looking at the dresses or colour options. She then had a problem with every dress she tried on varying from, it was the wrong colour, didn't like the material, didn't like the neckline.

I wanted to ask her if there was anything she did actually like, but I thought better of it.

The other two girls were starting to become uncomfortable with Stacey's persistent pessimism. They were happy if Elaine was happy and liked all of Elaine's choices for them—more like the sort of attitude you would expect from a bridesmaid. It was then, that Stacey abruptly informed Elaine that she would be deciding what she would be wearing if she was to be a bridesmaid. I thought *you can't even force yourself to show the slightest interest in the dresses but you've got the nerve to say you'll be deciding what you're wearing!* I was finding it difficult not to say exactly what I thought about her attitude. You could tell by this point that Stacey was just being deliberately negative and difficult. She was in danger of sabotaging the whole appointment with her behaviour, but I wasn't about to let that happen. So I decided to professionally intervene and asked Stacey, as her sister's chief bridesmaid aren't you just happy and honoured to be in this position? She had no response to this and just scowled at me. I can only imagine how she really wanted to respond to me.

It would seem that Stacey just couldn't see her sister happy—jealousy is a terrible thing, girls. If that's how she was behaving just now can you imagine her on the wedding day?

I think some sisters should remember, being asked to be your sister's bridesmaid is not an entitlement, it's a privilege.

Me, me—me!

Another bridesmaid appointment, another gaggle of girls. Vanessa the bride, three bridesmaids, mum and auntie. Chloe was the bridesmaid who became memorable that day. She was a very striking looking and confident girl. She stood out immediately from the group, so much so that I actually thought she was the bride and planning the wedding.

Vanessa hadn't chosen her wedding dress yet, but wanted to get her bridesmaids sorted out first. So the girls started to look through the dresses. Chloe really enjoyed this and she had a clear picture of what she wanted in her dress: the colour, style, shape and material. *Hopefully, Vanessa and the other two bridesmaids would share her vision too* I thought to myself.

So, into the dressing room, Chloe had to go first then the other two girls, all into dresses. They all looked lovely in pale blue one shoulder chiffon dresses, with a delicate sparkly belt. However, the conversation quickly started to revolve around Chloe, and how she felt and looked in the dress. She went on to tell everyone it had to make the most of her figure as everyone was going to be looking at her. She also described in detail how her hair and make-up would have to be done to highlight her best features. If this girl was made of chocolate, she would definitely eat herself! It's not exactly a comfortable situation having to listen to someone blowing their own trumpet, certainly not to this extent.

During this all about Chloe speech, the other two bridesmaids looked at each other as if to say, *does she need to be a bridesmaid.*

The dress that the girls decided on, (I should say Chloe decided on for them) was a bit out of Vanessa's price range. While she was quietly trying to discuss finances with her mum, Chloe got her eye on a large sparkly tiara.

It was then that Chloe announced that she was going to also need a tiara, "Might as well," she said. Then came one of the most self-obsessed things I've ever heard. Chloe said, "I mean when you look as good as I do, only the best will do. Cheap just doesn't look good on me. Let's face it, I do look the best in this dress out of the three of us—as she looked across at the other girls while now wearing the giant sparkly tiara—so it definitely has to be this one for me."

My jaw just dropped open and I think I might have gasped! I was actually embarrassed for her. *I thought is this girl for real, she must be joking?* Absolutely no shame.

The other two girls were squirming in their dresses. Vanessa's mum and auntie looked furious. It was then I decided to get the girls out of their dresses, let them have a little think and make a decision. By decision I was hoping for all their sakes to decide to get rid of Chloe. Or, at the very least, have this girl taken down a peg or two.

So, although being a bridesmaid is an important role to have, it's not more important than the bride on the big day.

So brides choose your bridesmaids wisely, even sisters and best friends are not guaranteed to be stress free.

The Body Beautiful

I don't think I've dressed a bride yet that was completely happy with her figure or didn't like some aspect of her body shape. In a world obsessed with image, it can make a girl fail to see her own natural beauty.

I have loved dressing brides of every shape and size and helping them to see how beautiful they are. I work in a shop that caters for all figures so that every bride, no matter what her dress size, can have a wonderful bridal experience.

Yo-yo

Although we stock a range of sizes in sample dresses, a large percentage of girls are slimming and want to lose weight before the wedding day.

Nichola was one of those brides. She said she found it difficult to maintain her weight. She also had an added health problem which made her retain water and caused her weight to fluctuate a lot.

Nichola was not very confident or positive during her appointment and had no faith that she could look or feel wonderful on her wedding day.

She picked out dresses that flattered her figure and we started to try them on. Throughout the dress tries, Nichola started to see that she had plenty of options and that alterations could be made if needed to accommodate any changes in her measurements and to make her feel comfortable.

She found a dress and wanted to come back with her mum and sister before making a final decision. She came back the following month with her mum and sister, but due to her medical condition she had gained a significant amount of weight since the last appointment.

As expected, when she tried on the dress again, it didn't fit so well. I was really disappointed for Nichola especially after the last time, she was feeling good about herself.

Her mum and sister were very supportive, saying: "not to worry, we know these things can happen, things will settle again."

Obviously, Nichola did not share their confidence. I explained that a corset back could be put into the dress to allow for changes.

Nichola still looked lovely in the dress but she couldn't see past the fact that if her weight fluctuated nearer the wedding, she wouldn't feel lovely.

Even though Nichola didn't feel the greatest on the day, she ordered the dress with a bit of persuasion from her mum and sister. While Nicholas dress was being made and before it arrived in the shop, Nichola had been seeing her doctor, dietician and had started personal training sessions. Nichola felt that she still had excess weight to lose even though she had a medical problem. She admitted that she would comfort eat and blame all her problems on her condition. So she decided to make some positive changes.

Nicholas dress arrived in the shop. I couldn't wait to see her in it and I also wanted to know how she was doing with her new healthy lifestyle.

When the door opened, I had to do a double take. I almost didn't recognise her. She had lost weight, had a new hair style, different style of clothes and make-up. Like a new woman. She looked amazing, happy and confident.

She explained about seeking health advice and that she also had some counselling sessions which helped her realise she was the one who had the power to take control, not her condition. With the positive changes, she had made up her mind that she was going to stay in control.

Nichola looked fantastic in her dress but more importantly as she said, "I feel fantastic." She still had her beautiful curves and was now positive and confident about her body.

It really goes to show girls that no matter how you look to others, it's about how you feel about yourself that's important.

Fighting Fit

It's not just girls who want to lose weight that can be body conscious. Girls who are on the slim side have issues too.

Sara was in her mid-thirties about 5'9" tall and a very slim build. Since her early teens, she had suffered from an eating disorder. Her weight had plummeted to life threatening levels and she had spent a lot of time in hospitals and rehabilitation clinics.

Sara's mum was a lovely woman, very supportive but you could see Sara's illness had taken its toll on her. I can only imagine the impact it would have on a mother with her daughter suffering from an illness like this.

Sara told how she was aware of the areas that she still felt were too slim and would choose dresses accordingly. She was not afraid to say what styles wouldn't flatter her and if a certain style made her look 'too skinny' as she put it. She was quite open about talking about how she looked. She was under no illusions as she looked through the dresses.

Sara reminded me that you shouldn't judge a book by its cover. Outwardly, she looked frail and weak but inside she was anything but. I could tell within a short time of talking to her that, although she had suffered from this illness for a long time, she had not lost her fighting spirit. Neither did she seem the kind of person that would suffer fools gladly, which was understandable considering what she'd been through in her lifetime. She was very direct and had no time for nonsense.

She described her illness as a constant fight to stay alive. She now felt that she had control and for the past four years was improving more and more. She sounded determined and positive about her future.

Time to get her into the dresses. Sara looked wonderful in the dresses and, yes, she still had a very slim figure but in the correct dresses, she just shone. Her mum was stunned with how great she looked and Sara couldn't believe how good she felt.

At this point, she had a little break to have a bulk up shake and a snack. She explained how she was trying to increase her snacking intake in between meals.

When Sara did find her perfect dress, she remained very calm and focused. She chose a fit and flare dress with a boat neckline and lace sleeves. It was a perfect choice for her figure and she felt really good in it. Her mum looked tearful, was very quiet and just sat watching her as Sara stood there. I didn't want to say anything to Sara's mum in case I upset her, and just let them have this quiet moment together.

They left together with Sara's mum thanking me so much for a wonderful experience. I was just happy to have been able to help Sara find a dress she loved and felt great in.

I can't imagine how difficult it must have been to battle with such a terrible illness for so long, but I was glad to see that Sara was winning the fight for her life.

Boobilicious

I don't think I can write a section on body image without talking about the drama us ladies have with our boobs. (Also referred to as, bangers, puppies, baps, the girls, tits, bazonkas etc). Getting up close and personal with girls in the changing room, I've found that around 90% of the time girls have issues with their boobs. They've tried all the tricks of the trade to conceal or enhance what they already have. From wonderbras to minimisers, multiway straps to chicken fillets.

Now, there had been a lot of memorable chats about boobs during appointments, but Vicky's solution to her boob issue was a bit more extreme.

Vicky had a great personality. She was really down to earth as was her mum during the appointment. Vicky had already looked at lot of dresses and had a good idea of what she wanted. It didn't take her long to decide on a dress: her favourite was a full satin skirt dress with train and a very detailed bodice with delicate sparkly straps.

She looked great in it but Vicky felt her boobs were too small and it was putting her off the dress. Her mum was trying to convince her that she looked fab and it didn't matter about the size of her boobs.

We could see Vicky was mulling it over in her head. After a few moments, she asked her mum to pass her phone so she could speak to her dad. I presumed to tell him she'd found a dress as he was maybe buying it for her.

This conversation did not go how I expected it to;

Vicky, "Hiya dad, it's me. I'm standing here in the bridal shop in this dress and it's the one I want, I really love it."

Dad: "Ok, that's great. Well, you just get whatever you want."

Vicky "Just one problem, I'll need to get these tits sorted out dad. I'll need to get a boob job. You should see the state of them, they're just too wee. So I'm wanting to order this dress but only if you'll pay for me to get these tits done."

I just looked at her mum, my mouth hanging open and my eyes wide. Her mum unphased by this request said, "I bet he'll just tell her to do whatever she wants."

Sure enough, Vicky's dad's response was, "Just whatever you think darling, I'll talk to you about it later." To which Vicky simply said, "Ok, see you later dad." Like it was a done deal.

I don't think I have or will ever hear a father daughter conversation like that again. It was as if she was asking him if he wanted to come over and have a cup of tea. So matter of fact about it. Her dad was obviously as relaxed as her mum.

So Vicky ordered her dress and was off to book her boob job appointment. I don't know if she ever did go through with it but either way, she looked fab in her dress and was going to have a blast at her wedding.

I don't think I'd be so brave to go for the permanent option but 'each to their own' on this one.

I would hope that in the future more women can learn to embrace their bodies and if you are really unhappy with something, take control and make a positive change. Or just do what Vicky did: phone your dad to pay for boob job!

Wedding Fayres

Another part of my job involves working at wedding fayres. I've worked in lots of different venues over the years from stadiums to town halls and hotels. I really enjoy working at these events. I get to meet lots of great people who are all looking forward to their wedding days still to come.

There is often a catwalk at these events where I get the chance to model all the different styles of wedding dresses. I am obviously in my element while doing this. I just love being a bride and having the chance to wear all these beautiful dresses.

There are two standout stories that took place at wedding fayres which I've chosen to share with you.

No matter how hard I try, I can't forget them. As both of them involve me being completely, mortified!

Granny Takedown

This story took place at a very large wedding fayre, a full weekend event. I had already worked all day on Saturday and was back to work on Sunday. I was a bit tired from standing all day on the Saturday but I put my face on, did my hair and got my dress on to work at my stand.

I was wearing quite a full dress that day, a jacquard material with quite a big skirt, really comfortable though which was good as I had to be in it all day.

I had been giving out leaflets and promotional information all day with another girl called Ailey, who used to work part-time with us. She was wearing a sapphire blue satin bridesmaids dress with a dipped hem and looked beautiful in it.

I had talked to hundreds of people that weekend, and a lot of people had commented on the dresses we were wearing. Which is the purpose of us being in bridal wear while we work at fayres, so that people can the see the dresses on 'real' people.

I was just finishing speaking to a group of girls who were walking away from me when I turned around to see an elderly lady walking towards me smiling. She looked like she was in her seventies, immaculately presented in her lilac twin set and pearls. She had silver bird brooch on her cardigan and her handbag over her arm. I looked in her direction thinking she's going to be lovely to have a wee chat with. (Oh how deceiving looks can be) She then said in a voice loud, enough to be heard by nearby exhibitors and people walking past, "Aw, what a difference that is to see an older bride in a wedding dress!" It took me a few seconds for it to dawn on me that she was actually speaking about me. I was 35 years old at the time and never before considered that I was getting older.

She went on, "You look just as lovely as those younger girls, hen." She then shouted to her daughter to come and see me in this dress and continued, "look, this lassies older and she looks braw." Then, "She's no skinny either, see you don't have to be thin to get married!" My god, just give this woman a shovel! I wanted the ground to open up and swallow me whole. I mean, who actually says that to someone? Never mind shout it from a distance!

Meanwhile Ailey is hiding behind her clipboard trying to conceal her laughter. I could see all the other exhibitors looking at me and feeling my pain. She just didn't seem to read my facial expression of being totally gutted. If ever I've had a back handed compliment in my life, that was it.

I can barely even remember how I responded to her, something like, "Well people get married at different stages in their life." I was trying to keep it light hearted and hide the fact she had just shattered me.

It's a good job I'm thick skinned! I did recover from her insult/compliment though and was able to laugh about it with Ailey all the way home. If I'd been a more sensitive type person, I would maybe have taken from her comments that it was time to start losing weight and get some botox!

So for future fayres, I remember to stay on my guard when a see a smiling granny coming towards me.

Watch Your Step

On this occasion, we were exhibiting at a hotel and showcasing our dresses on the catwalk.

We had teamed up with the kilt hire exhibitors that day, which we often do to catwalk together.

We had already done a few rounds of walking the catwalk, individually, and then we were going to walk down as couples. I was to walk with David, a guy I've walked with for years. He's a bit older than me and we kinda look like a father and daughter walking together. He's been trying to give me away for years!

We always have a great laugh. The guys have really good fun on the catwalk, making the audience laugh with their antics.

It was time for David and I to walk together. I usually walk down the catwalk first while David waits at the top, then he walks down while I wait, and then we walk together.

We've done this loads of times before so it wasn't anything new. I'd just walked down the catwalk, done my turns and posed for the camera, and was standing at the end of the catwalk watching David.

He was getting a good laugh from the crowd by swishing his kilt about for them.

Then everything went into slow motion for me. I think I was distracted by David and wasn't paying attention to where I was. I forgot I was standing on the catwalk and took a step back! I thought, *Oh no, it's actually happening I'm falling off the catwalk!* The thing I've always dreaded that could happen to me was actually happening right now. Worst nightmare!

David was now on his way back up to me and he could see the fear in my face as I was now in mid fall. He ran with his arm extended to and grab me, but I was too far away. I was already gone. I was filled with horror as I waited to land on a group of women in the front row.

By some miracle my step back landed firmly on the ground and I managed to recover my balance to gasps from everyone around me. Honestly, it was like something out the Matrix!

David pulled me back onto the catwalk and we just walked off together. I now had to do a quick dress change and get back out there. I was so embarrassed and still in shock! I could not believe that had just happened. How could I go back out there after that disaster? My heart was pounding, my face bright red and I was now in a huge ball gown. I just wanted to run away, I was shaking like a leaf and my bottom lip was trembling.

I stepped out and David was waiting for me on the catwalk. He took my hand to help me up and said to the whole crowd, "A round of applause, please?" to which they all responded to with cheering and clapping as I took a bow, did a curtsy and continued my walk to a standing ovation.

I just couldn't believe it, mortified is an understatement. If I hadn't laughed, I would have cried but as they say,

"The Show Must Go On."

Runaway Brides

With all the planning, pressures and stress of organising a wedding it's no wonder that some couples choose to elope.

This has become an increasingly popular option for couples in recent years. For those who have family issues, religious differences, financial uncertainty or simply want to say their vows to each other on their own. Choosing to elope can be a perfect option for some couples.

Society and traditions do tend to dictate what you "have to have" at your wedding, which a lot of the time is not meaningful to the couple. By deciding to elope the couple can escape all this and have a ceremony that is beautiful and completely personal to them.

Young Love

Tracey and John, husband to be, came to Tracey's bridal appointment together. They were a youngish couple in their early twenties.

They were planning to elope so there would only be the two of them on their special day. As they were planning their wedding in secret, they only had each other to talk to about it and Tracey wanted John by her side while choosing the dress.

They had decided to elope because their parents weren't supportive of their engagement and said they were too young to be married, but they thought otherwise.

Tracey was quite excited about it all. I could tell she hadn't been able to talk to anyone else about the wedding the way she was telling me all about it. She was almost whispering all the details to me as if not to say it too loudly, in case somehow it might spoil their secret. She kept saying how it didn't feel 'real', like they were just pretending to get married.

She hoped that once she saw herself in the dresses, it would become more real.

John was quite laid back and relaxed but very set in their decision to elope. He had no reservations about it at all. It was lovely to see that no matter what his family's thoughts were, he knew he loved Tracey and wanted to marry her. As did she.

Although they were considered to be a young couple, they had been together since high school and known each other all their lives. At the age of five years old, they started primary school together. They can barely remember each other not being there. So they both knew exactly how the other one felt.

They were such a lovely couple and I felt sorry for them that their families couldn't be supportive. I also wondered how their families would react when they found out about the wedding.

Tracey started to look at all the dresses and John had a seat and waited to see her in them. Tracey picked out six or seven dresses that she liked, and we started to try them on. After about four dresses, she found one she really liked: bohemian style, floaty with delicate lace detailing. She also tried on a simple veil with it. She stood in front of the mirrors and looked at herself for a few minutes. I could see she was absorbing the moment. She turned to John and said, "It feels real now." This was to be Tracey's dress. John agreed, she looked lovely in it and thought she should go for it.

Tracey just loved it, and didn't want to take it off. As she was standing there, I thought *had their parents been on side with their decision to marry they all would see how stunning Tracey looked in her dress.*

This didn't seem to matter to John or Tracey, they didn't seek approval from anyone and very much felt that their wedding was for them.

Tracey left delighted that day with her dress. I really do wish them all the best for the future. I was happy to see that they were doing what they wanted to do and weren't pushed out of their decision by other people.

So even if you don't have family support on your side and you do choose to go it alone, your wedding day will always be special to you.

25 years Later

Another couple that chose to elope were Susan and Greg. They were planning to get married but could really have been planning their silver wedding as they'd already been together for 25 years.

They'd already shared a life together, brought up children, and now had grandchildren. They said they had always wanted to get married but just "never got round to it". They now felt it was time to seal the deal. I thought this was so lovely.

A wedding can often be at the start of a couple's life together but for Susan and Greg, it was to be a continuation of their story, a new chapter if you like.

They were planning a simple ceremony and were telling no-one. With personalised vows, which included precious moments from their life together and new hopes for the future. They were still very happy and content with each other, after all these years. Susan said that by getting married it would just cement what they already had.

They chose to elope because they simply did not want a fuss. They felt they had already enjoyed lots of special moments with family and friends over the years and they just wanted it to be the two of them on their wedding day.

Susan was unsure at first if she was going to have a wedding dress, and said that it was Greg who persuaded her to go and try some on.

She was glad she did. She loved trying on the dresses and looked great in them. I was glad she was enjoying her bridal experience.

She chose an A-line chiffon dress with lace capped sleeves. She also added a little sparkly belt to the waistline. It looked lovely on her and she looked natural and comfortable in it. I was glad she chose to wear a dress, she was going to look beautiful on her wedding day. She told me that she was going to wear jewellery that Greg had given to her over the years on special occasions, from when their children were born and from their first Christmas together. So lovely to bring all those memories together for their wedding day.

I'm sure Susan and Greg had a lovely ceremony together and had the day they wanted, minus the fuss that they didn't want.

I think how blessed Susan and Greg were to have already shared a wonderful life together. I wish them well for the future. Here's to the next 25 years!

My Turn

So I've saved this story to last, as you can guess from the title, it's my story!

We were also one of the couples who chose to elope for our wedding ceremony. Scott, my now husband, and I decided to elope along with our son and two friends as witnesses.

We knew that we could not have everyone at our wedding that we wanted. After having lost a parent to illness myself, and Scott now having a parent with an illness which would mean they would be unable to attend, it lead us to thinking about a more private ceremony.

Also, Scott and I did not feel that we had to say our vows in front of anyone else to make them more meaningful to us. Our ceremony and vows were tailored to be personal to us and we really felt that we wanted to keep that special moment for ourselves. Our son was even included in the vows, and we presented him with his own little wedding ring.

We chose a place to marry that held special childhood memories for me. We were married by a registrar in the forest near waterfalls in a place called Aberfeldy.

I wore an ivory, one shoulder chiffon dress with a full length veil and carried a large rustic bouquet of green foliage and gypsophlia. I felt so happy and relaxed, floating around the forest in my wedding dress. I loved my dress and felt amazing in it. I felt a bit like a character from a secret garden or a fairy story.

It was late September so not too warm, but I thought it was perfect. The sun beamed between the trees during our ceremony and as we had photos taken. I remember feeling like I was in a dream, like this wasn't really happening. I kept having to remind myself that I'd just got married! It really was perfect for us and I wouldn't have changed a thing. It was lovely, really peaceful and serene, such a beautiful ceremony. It was quite surreal standing in the forest in my wedding dress while hikers and dog walkers were passing by and congratulating us.

When we got back to our hotel and it had started to sink in that we had just taken our vows, we face timed everyone to tell them the news, that was fun! Spoke to a few chosen family members and friends, and then texted some photos to everyone else. Although some people would have loved to have been there with us, they were delighted for us.

Not being content with planning a secret ceremony, I also planned a Part 2 to our wedding celebrations, which was to take place a few months later. Although I was glad we had a private ceremony, I still wanted to celebrate our marriage.

We had all of our family and friends present, another wedding dress, bridesmaids, boys in kilts, meal and speeches, wedding cake, big reception, the whole shabang!

This time I wore something completely different. It was a full ball gown, duchess satin skirt with train, which had little buttons all the way down the back. It was a heavily embellished sweetheart bodice with embellished illusion neckline and back. The bead work on it was exceptional. It also had a sparkly belt which pulled it in at the waist, complete with a full length single tier veil with sparkly lace edging. I had to have a veil, I love veils. The dress was stunning and I felt like royalty in it! It really did have an impact.

We all had a fantastic day and night together, we also had a hand fastening blessing and photo shoot in the grounds of the estate. We kinda had the whole wedding but without the added pressure of a ceremony and saying our vows in front of everyone.

I enjoyed Part 2 from start to finish. As I look over my wedding photos from both weddings again and again, I really am delighted with the decisions we made and have no regrets.

I'm not sure if other girls have experienced this, but have you ever heard people tell you what "you'll have to have and have to do" when they hear you're planning a wedding? Well, as soon as someone told me I'd need to do something, it just made me question why, "Says who?" I chose to do the opposite of what people said I had to do. It was when we decided not to try and please others that we were able to plan another wonderful day.

When planning the most important day of your life, (or days in my case) you want to remember it because it was wonderful, not regret that you didn't do it your way.

I wish all you future couples a magical wedding day and hope that it is all you dreamed of.

Do what is right for you both and above all remember it's the marriage that's important. Once the wedding day fades, your marriage will remain and grow.

Afterword

When I started working in a bridal shop, I never expected there to be such variation in what might happen during appointments. I've found that I became very involved with brides and their families during this time. Some people were very open and this made it very easy to connect with them.

I've learned that connections and relationships with others are vital for a happy and successful life. Be it for the duration of an appointment or for the rest of your life with your loved ones. We need to be able to get along.

I've always been a people person and I am genuinely interested in people's life experiences and what they have to say.

I've met some wonderful people and as I've said are now 'unforgettable' to me. I wonder if I've had the same lasting impact on them!

I've enjoyed revisiting these chosen ones while writing this book and think, it will be clear to see why they have become embedded in my brain! I hope to be working with brides for many more years and I'm sure there will be plenty more memorable moments to come.

To be continued…

Ingram Content Group UK Ltd.
Milton Keynes UK
UKHW021849280423
420960UK00007B/36